WORKBOOK

For

HOW TO
BE AN
ANTIRACIST

By

IBRAM X. KENDI

Made Press

Table of Contents

ABOUT THE AUTHOR

IBRAM X. KENDI is a public speaker and columnist at The Atlantic. H
is an outstanding New York Times bestselling author who is the bra
behind the Antiracist Research and Policy Center at the America
University. IBRAM X. KENDI resides in Washington, D.C., and
professor of history and international relations. He is the author o
"The Black Campus Movement", which won the W.E.B. Du Bois Boc
Prize and "Stamped from the Beginning: The Definitive History o
Racist Ideas in America" that won the National Book Award fo
Nonfiction.

MY RACIST INTRODUCTION

The author; IBRAM X. KENDI sequentially narrates an array of events that reveals what led him to gain so much confidence in himself at a tender age and how a simple academic oratorical contest contributed tremendously, ushering him to being the best version of himself. For a long time, he thought himself unintelligent and silly. He uncompromisingly used his academic performance to gauge his intellectual ability which was very wrong, until he found his niche and has never been this efficacious since then.

A reflection that comes to mind from that experience made him wonder if it was his poor sense of self that brought about his poor sense of people OR his poor sense of people that ignited his poor sense of self? The idea behind racism makes people of color feel less of themselves thereby making them susceptible to racist ideas. On the other hand, racist ideas make Whites feel more of themselves and further attract them to more racist ideas. The media, TV shows, Whites, and other Black people further made me think Black people weren't intellectual. As years passed the society hardened the racist ideas residing in me and caused me to speak up.

For many years we have been allocating racist ideas about our people to our people; we have been going about ending racism in the very wrong way. Imagine me arming up and shooting at the very people I should have to protect with my unguarded misdirection of racist ideas. It is now common to practice internalized racism which is an absolute display of Black on Black crime without being aware we are doing just that. This racist idea makes us see ourselves as the problem and not the policies the society forces us to abide by. A typical example is the forty-fifth president of the United States; Donald Trump who stops at nothing to speak ill of the people of color. When accused of being a racist, he swings into denial mode. This isn't surprising as that is the very heartbeat of racism – "denial".

There is a strong concern with claiming not to be racist. The concern is neutrality. So you claim not to be racist but you do nothing to end racism. In my honest opinion, that automatically makes you racist. You are either racist or antiracist; neutrality isn't the opposite of racism! Racism is very descriptive and not pejorative as many think it to be. The idea behind painting it as a pejorative word is to make the people of color inactive in the pursuit of ending racism. Another method of covert racism is hiding behind the curtain of "not being racist to cover up being racist" that is color blindness. This is the act of claiming not to see skin tones, failing to recognize a specific race leading to racist passivity. It's a shame that the white constitution is color-blind – Justice John Harlan revealed this.

Due to the constant movement of racial sides (racist/anti-racist) it brings to limelight the need to understand race based on the following – culture, biology, body, ethnicity, behavior, class, color, and space. Putting a permanent end to racism is a possibility if we focus on the racial power and not the people – if we drag our attention to altering policies in place of the community and be optimistic about the prolonged existence of racism. We can learn to be anti-racist just the way we learned to be racist and pretend not to be racist.

CHAPTER 1: DEFINITIONS

A racist is an individual who encourages or perpetuates racist policies through their actions or inaction or via racist ideas. While an antiracist is an individual who practices antiracist policies through their actions or affirming antiracist ideas.

Soul liberation crusade ushered in a new dawn of radical evolutionary. Tom skinner, an evangelist – formerly got the wrong image of Jesus Christ. He perceived Him to be an elite not knowing He was down to earth radical revolutionary. His previous preachings before this realization supported slavery, segregation and said it is a taboo for any black man to stand without a white man aiding it. Skinner's orientation changed as he spread the gospel issues bothering on enslavement, injustice, and inequality. Skinner went further to gather evangelical liberators for the Black cause.

Black Power movement for Black cultural pride, Black solidarity, Black economic and political freedom grew more in the 1950s and 1960s in the days of Malcolm X, Stokely Carmichael, Fannie Lou Hamer, and other antiracists who opposed assimilationists and segregationists. James Cone, the scholarly father of Black liberation theology and writer of the influential "Black Theology & Black Power" in 1969 defined Christianity as one striving for freedom. This reality of Christianity turned racists and passive racist to antiracists.

Racism is the matrimony of racist ideas and racist policies in other to create and regularize racial inequities. Racial inequality is a situation whereby two or more racial groups are not standing on an equal pedestal. The racist policy is any decree that encourages racial

inequality amongst racial groups while the antiracist policy is tha
which boosts racial equity amongst racial groups.

Racism is institutional, systemic, and structural. Raci
discrimination is a notable display of fundamental racial policy. Th
sort of discrimination is fueled by the lack of protective policy in plac
which is perpetuated by racist policymakers (racist power). Raci
discrimination can bring about equity and inequity, depending on th
motive driving it. Racial discrimination can be nipped in the bud b
hiring antiracist discrimination. The idea of race neutrality nurse
White nationalist victimhood in the sense that any idea politicizin
the protection and propagation of people of color to equity
"reverse discrimination." This is just a sheer show of racist power.
sees any act of reducing racial inequality as being "race-conscious
and that which in turn promotes racial inequality as "race-neutral."

Racist ideas are notions suggesting a racial group is inferior c
superior to others while antiracist ideas uphold that racial groups ar
equal and none is more superior to the other. Antiracist ideas pos
that racist policies are the main reason for racial inequalities.
Kendi illustrated how he lost his maternal grandmother t
Alzheimer's and grandfather to cancer, diseases mostly suffered b
African Americans. He explained that White privilege places Whit
lives on a scale of 3.5 more years over Black lives in the U.S.

Racists or antiracists are not permanent tattoos. No one is bor
to be any of the aforementioned terms. It takes one to intentional t
be any of them, persistence, continual self-criticism, and daily self
evaluation. In the face of your conviction to be radically antiracist
calls for a radical reorientation of your consciousness.

- **Lessons**

1. Racism is descriptive and not a pejorative word.
2. A racist is an individual who encourages or perpetuates racist policies through their actions or inaction or via racist ideas. While an antiracist is an individual who practices antiracist policies through their actions or stating an antiracist idea.
3. Racism is a matrimony of racist ideas and racist policies in other to create and regularize racial inequities
4. No one is a born racist or antiracist, our society forms us into being one.

- **Issues surrounding the subject matter**
  1. Have you ever been considered a racist and why?

  _____

  _____

  _____

  _____

  _____

  2. What are the emotions you feel when tagged a racist?

  _____

  _____

  _____

  _____

  _____

  3. How it is that racial discrimination is relative?

  _____

  _____

  _____

  _____

- **Goals**

1. How do you intend to make sure your racial discrimination propagates equity and not inequity?

_____

_____

_____

_____

_____

_____

_____

_____

_____

_____

2. How do you intend to not be defensive and emit other related emotions when called a racist by a person of color?

_____

_____

_____

_____

_____

_____

_____

_____

_____

3. How do you intend to speak to individuals immersed by White supremacy about the injustice and inequality and be granted a listening ear?

_____

_____

_____

_____

_____

_____

_____

_____

_____

_____

- **Action steps**
  1. In this work, you have you involved others interested in antiracism to help propagate the gospel. You can do it alone but it is of more motivation and impact when supported by like minds.
- **Checklist**
  1. Antiracism requires perseverance and doggedness to overcome.

CHAPTER 2: DUELING CONSCIOUSNESS

An assimilationist is one whose racial beliefs is that a raci[al] group is culturally or behaviorally inferior and therefore begins th[e] journey of restoring the dignity of that race by embarking on cultur[al] or behavioral development programs for that racial group.

A segregationist has a racist idea that a perpetually inferior raci[al] group will never be developed, so they support policies that furth[er] isolates them.

An antiracist is one with an idea that racial groups are equa[l] not needing development and support policies that reduce raci[al] inequality.

The author, born in 1982 when President Reagan's regim[e] called for stricter judgment on drug-related crimes. This caused [a] spike in the prison cell bringing up the percentage of Africa[n] Americans to 53% more likely to be imprisoned during the sam[e] length of time for a more violent crime committed by White[s] thereby bringing their percentage to approximately 30% in the yea[r] 1980 to 2000. Other American leaders like the above that mad[e] policies to suffer and cripple the Black community in the past wer[e] President Lyndon B. Johnson in 1965, President Richard Nixon i[n] 1971, and Bill Clinton just to shut the mouths of the people of colo[r]. To make matters worse, Black leaders contributed to the slander jus[t] to look like saviors while destroying the image of members of th[e] black community.

As this era's projected Black vilification, it also called for the end o[f] Police brutality, better schools, better job opportunities, and drug treatment programs. But as expected, the demands of the Blac[k] community was taken for levity. By 1982 the Black on Black crime was at the peak and we became a thing of mockery to the Whites and to even some of the Blacks. The civil-rights lawyer – Eleanor Holmes Norton published on The New York times that the solution doesn't lie only in giving the necessities and opportunities the People of color clamor for; but asked that the "Black ghetto subculture" be crumbled. This call was to parents and guardians with "ghetto blood" to look into their origin and save their ghetto males/females, urge them to be more hardworking, respectful, aspire for academic gains, and want more out of life. The focus was now on the family chastising their wards to be better and more responsible and that spread across the Black community.

We all forgot that there are policies in the society that hinders us from getting very far no matter how hard we try. These policies have been in place even before we were conceived. So while we were striving to be the best versions of ourselves, the institutions put in place by the government kept pulling us back and frustrating our efforts. The Reagan revolution is a very typical example. His reign was a radical uprising that benefited only the powerful. Made the wealthy whites richer by chopping off their taxes and government regulations, set up a Christmas-tree military budget, and detained the power of unions. In 1979 the rate of racial discrimination rose tremendously and many Blacks were driven into deeper poverty due to the slashing of the federal welfare program gains and medic aid. Also, his stricter law enforcement made more Blacks susceptible to fall into the hands of violent cops that killed twenty-two Blacks for every White person in the 1980s. Unemployment was also on the rise as Blacks suffered to put food on their table or cater for their family needs.

The Whites have been schooled to see the deficiencies of people rather than paying a closer look at the policy. Members of the Black community started trying so hard to fit into the White space in other to be accepted and enjoy the same benefits as the Whites. This led to double-consciousness as labeled by W.E.B. Du Bois in The Souls of Black Folk in 1903. Du Bois explained how he wanted to be both American and Negro at the same, but it didn't work because being American at the same time as White is not Negro. This leads us to duel consciousness. The longing to enjoy the White privilege and also be Negro is the struggle behind dueling consciousness. Du Bios believed in the antiracist concept of racial dependence and the assimilationist concept of racial standards. While the former looks at oneself with its own eyes, the latter looks at oneself through the eyes of another racial group (White people). So in a bid to free Black people from racism, there is a need for change to protect them from their savagery leftovers.

Assimilationists put the Whites as the main racial group with superior standards that other racial groups should emulate. But what metrics was that assimilation founded on? What makes them the superior race? Should there even be a thing as a superior race? Assimilationist ideas are racist.

The dueling consciousness births Black self-reliance which is a double-edged sword. One end abhors White supremacy, White rulers, and White saviorism of White paternalism while the other end dotes on Black rulers and Black saviors of Black paternalism. The ueling consciousness believes that nothing is wrong with the Black race and we are capable of ruling and relying on ourselves. Although Blacks need to put a check on their behavior while the assimilationist thinks otherwise.

Whites also go through dueling consciousness between the segregationist and the assimilationist, e.g. between the Blue Lives Matter and the All Lives Matter (the proslavery exploiter and the antislavery civilizer)… Segregationist ideas and assimilationist ideas are the two kinds of racist ideas in the minds of racist. White assimilationist ideas defy segregationist ideas saying that people of color are not capable of development, gaining superior standards, being White, and a complete human. Assimilationists believe that people of color can be developed and recognized as humans.

Assimilationist's policies veer towards developing, integrating, and civilizing the racial group. While segregationist policies talk about the inability of a racial group to be developed and civilized thus encouraging segregating policies, enslavement, deportation, incarceration, and killings. The dueling white consciousness has shaped the tussle within Black consciousness from a relative power position. There is a strong desire to be Black and White both at the same time. The desire to be White lays on White privilege, freedom from police violence, voters dominance, health insurance, etc. Unconsciously the Whites force their frame on the Blacks. They are ordered to act, talk, and think like the Whites as that is the accepted way of doing things. But the Blacks never imposes anything on the Whites. Be antiracist today and free yourself from the dueling

consciousness, assimilationist consciousness, and the segregationi
consciousness.

- **Lessons**
    1. The policies are the problem and not the people.
    2. Antiracist ideas are built on the truth that racial groups a
       all equal in all their unique disparities.
    3. Assimilationist ideas are grounded in the concept th.
       certain racial groups are behaviorally or culturally inferio
    4. Segregationist ideas are believed to come from genet
       racial distinction and fixed hierarchy.
- **Issues surrounding the subject matter**
    1. What is the idea behind the assimilationist policies and th
       segregationist policies as it bothers on race?

_____

_____

_____

_____

_____

_____

- **Goals**
    1. Did you or your parents also fall victim to striving to sav
       and civilize your fellow Black people rather than liberat
       them and how did that turn out?

_____

_____

_____

_____

_____

_____

_____

_____

_____

_____

2. How do you think you can free yourself from the dueling consciousness?

_____

_____

_____

_____

_____

_____

_____

_____

_____

- **Action steps**
  1. To be antiracist requires dropping a lot of baggage you have stocked up in your mind, drop them off and move on.
- **Checklist**
  1. Until we begin to see that the White body no longer prides itself as the American body and the Black body stops striving to be the American body, (as there is nothing like that) then we haven't started.

CHAPTER 3: POWER

Race can be defined as a power construct of merge differences living socially. The author noted how he got to racia puberty at a very young age of seven. He attained this through th help of his father who drowned him in biographies by Black leaders These materials made him racially sound. At that age, he was alread consumed by the powerful construction of race. Nevertheless, th race is just an illusion which doesn't reduce its force. We are collection of what we see ourselves as even though it is present c not. We are what others see us as to whether what is seen exists c not. What people see in others and see in themselves has a lot c meaning and it shows in their policies, ideas, and actions, eve though it's all an illusion. Race is a mirage but it is the potent light c racist power that makes it phantasm.

Race has forced many to see themselves in various ways. Th author due to his experience sees himself culturally and politicall and historically Black even though he is an African American and member of the forced and unforced African diaspora. It is a rare gif to see oneself for what they truly are and in his case, he is Black an racial color-blindness hasn't gotten the best of him. As an antiracist he sees himself historically and politically as a member of the bod striving to empower racial equality.

In America, it is a racial crime to be yourself, look like yourself or get some sort of empowerment if you are not White. Race has th power to classify and judge, promote and demote, include, and exclude. Race creators make use of that power to process uniqu individualities, ethnicities, and nationalities into colossal races. Th first universal power to create race was the first racist power and the first private slave trader of the constructed race of African people named Prince Henry and nicknamed the "Navigator," even though he did not leave Portugal in the fifteenth century (as many may know). Henry opened up a portal of slavery that had never been before. His slavery advances spread to West Africa to the Islamic slave traders where he had his first major slave auction in Lagos, Portugal, in 1444. His legacy was continued by his royal chronicler and a loyal commander called Zurara in 1460 when Prince Henry died.

Race making is an indispensable component in the making of racist ideas. Once a race is created it has to be filled in. In 1735, Carl Linnaeus created the racial hierarchy of humanity in *Systema Naturae*. He used colors to symbolize a race, using White, Yellow, Red, and Black. This he did attaching each race to the four regions of the world according to their characteristics. They are the Homo sapiens europaeus topping the racial hierarchy, the Homo sapiens asiaticus, the Homo sapiens americanus, and Homo sapiens afer at the bottom of the racial hierarchy. This became a blueprint for most race makers even till date. Zurara posited that the slave trading was all in a bid to save souls and not to make money.

It is incorrect to say that a racist idea is the only cause of racist policies. Or that the core reason for racism is ignorance and hate. The real challenge of racism over time from the experience of past leaders to date shows that self-interest has a strong role to play in racist power.

- **Lessons**
  1. Race is a powerful construct of merged differences living socially.
  2. Race is just an illusion that doesn't relent on its force.
  3. Race is a mirage but it is the potent light of racist power that makes it phantasm.
- **Issues surrounding the subject matter**
  1. Would you agree that Powerful economic, political, and cultural self-interest is the key reason for racism and why?

  _____

  _____

  _____

  _____

  _____

  _____

  _____

  _____

  _____

  2. Did the founding fathers of the slave trade embark on slave trading just to save souls or what other underlined interest was involved?

  _____

  _____

  _____

  _____

  _____

  _____

- **Goals**

1. How do you intend to be a positive race maker with antiracism at heart?

_____

_____

_____

_____

_____

_____

_____

_____

_____

2. What is your take on how selfish-interest is the root cause of racism?

_____

_____

_____

_____

_____

_____

_____

_____

- **Action steps**
    1. Race makers don't define what race means to you, hold your culture dear to your heart, and don't lose it for anything.
- **Checklist**
    1. Race is a mirage.

CHAPTER 4: BIOLOGY

There are biological racist and biological antiracists. A biological racist is one who believes that races differ in their biology and these variances in race create a hierarchy of value. On the other hand, biological antiracists are one with the opinion that races are the same in their biology and there are no existing genetic racial variances.

People of color take maltreatment from Whites by hiding behind the Whiteness banner. It is dangerous to generalize a White racist behavior as an all-White thing and the same goes for generalizing the distinct fault of people of color to an entire race. We have all formed a habit of racist categorizing – seeing and remembering the race and not the individual in question. A renowned Harvard psychiatrist Chester Pierce coined a term called "microaggression" in 1970. The aforementioned term is used to describe the consistent verbal and nonverbal racial abuse the Whites dish out to Black people on end.

Here are some of the ways the Whites abuse Black people:

1. Assuming us to the help or that the help isn't brilliant.
2. A white woman gripping her purse at the sight of a Black.
3. Calling the cops on Black children for selling lemonade on the streets.
4. Calling the cops at the sight of Black people barbecuing in the park.
5. Taking Black firmness for anger.
6. Calling the cops on Blacks as they run down the street exercising.

Another psychologist in the person of Derald Wing Sue defined microaggressions as the momentary daily interactions that send demeaning messages to certain individuals because of where they come from. It thrives more in our supposedly post-racial era when we thought we saw a significant sign through the election of the first Black president. Race progressed and so did racism. Racism became less descriptive and more pejorative. Many Americans sort a less descriptive way to identify and propagate racism leading to – "microaggression." Words like cultural wars, tribalism, economic anxiety, stereotype, and implicit bias replaced racism as a word. Yes, racism still lingers in our society; the abuse of the People of color has become a constant and seems like no decline is in sight. This abuse causes anger, distress, worry, anxiety, depression, fatigue, pain, and even leads to suicidal tendencies.

In the face of all these abuses, there exist zero-tolerance policies that let these abusers go unpunished. Racism thrives on denial and that is what is flourishing in our world today. The silent treatment is given to victims of racial abuse and their families have to live in the horror of watching their loved ones violently taken away just because no one with White privilege or the White supremacist wouldn't speak up to defend them.

In school, White teachers treat Black children as adults. They don't use empathy and legitimacy; instead, they are commanded and punished for not complying with instructions forgetting that they also have blood running through their veins, but the White kids aren't treated as such. In several ways, superficial variances symbolized various forms of humanity which is the essence of biological racism. Biological racists are segregationists, their opinion of race is that races differ in their biology and these variances in race create a hierarchy of value. This conflicts with the biblical creation story of Adam and Eve being equals. So where did the grouping, variances, and inequality arise from? We can say there are different races biologically but it is out of place to say there is a biological racial hierarchy. Who made anyone the judge of categorizing human beings and placing them hierarchically? That is a racist alert! White blood and Black blood. How Blacks tend to be physically stronger than the White counterpart. How Blacks are natural improvisers. How Blacks are unintelligent and thrive in basic things and less intellectual activities like basketball playing, rap, jazz, and not it chess, astronomy, and classical music. How Black women are naturally endowed physically and Black men graciously gifted with large penises.

More biblical references were given as regards why Blacks were the race that suffered slavery and not any other. In 1578, English trave writer George Best tried in explaining from biblical terms that just maybe the Blacks happen to be the descendants of Ham (Noah's sor who he caused). Ham looked upon his father's nakedness and Noah learned of it and cursed his generation (Canaan) with slavery. Many Blacks believed that their slavery state was justified and that they are paying for the sins of their greatest grandfather (Ham). But this i very misleading as Number 14:18 doesn't hold water anymore nov Ezekiel 18:20 applies.

Biologist Charles Darwin posited in his publication: The Origin o Species in 1859, the theory of natural selection which is used t listinguish and rank the races. This theory supported that the only utcome for the "weaker" race was slavery, extinction, and ssimilation. But on June 26, 2000, Bill Clinton gave a speech eadlined: DECODING THE BOOK OF LIFE / A MILESTONE FOR HUMANITY. The summary and findings of that speech made us understand that all humans are more than 99.9% the same regardless of race. This makes modern science confirm that our ancient faith was on track. But these biological genetic findings were short-lived as soon as scientists announced the result of the second phase of their biological genetic findings and discovered that the human race is genetically different.

Linking biology to behavior is the origin of biological racism, thereby leading to biological race ranking and superiority behavioral traits. Racial ancestry doesn't exist but ethnic ancestry exists. There is only one race and that is the human race. A racist society imagines away the existence of races. This is as harmful as erasing the thoughts of classes in a capitalist world. Assimilationists believe that talking about race increases the chances of racism and if we stop talking about it; it will magically go away. Part of the solution is to stop racial categorizing then the rest will follow – racial inequality dies, racist policies die, challenging racist policies will be exterminated, then racist power will come to stay. That's a world free of inequality and discord.

- **Lessons**
  1. Biological racist thinks that races differ in their biology an these variances in race create a hierarchy of value.
  2. Biological antiracists believe that races are the same i their biology and there are no existing genetic racia variances.
  3. Race progressed and so did racism.
  4. Biological racists are segregationists, their opinion of rac is that races differ in their biology and these variances i race create a hierarchy of value.
- **Issues surrounding the subject matter**
  1. Have you ever been in a situation where you were terme a racist just because you discussed race and how did yo handle it?

  _____

  _____

  _____

  _____

  _____

  _____

  _____

  _____

  _____

  2. What is your view on the biological racial differences?

  _____

  _____

  _____

  _____

  _____

  _____

- **Goals**
  1. What is the best way to talk about race without being perceived as a racist?

  _____

  _____

  _____

  _____

  _____

  2. What is your honest opinion on racial inequality and how to enact the saying that "there is only one race and it is the human race?"

  _____

  _____

  _____

  _____

  _____

  3. What would you say is the origin of your biological racism, biological race ranking, and superiority behavioral trait and how can you do away with that vile idea?

  _____

  _____

  _____

  _____

  _____

- **Action steps**
  1. Talk more about race with Black people and White people so that they understand that race is descriptive; not talking about it won't let it go away, don't be fooled.
- **Checklist**
  1. The human race is the only race.

CHAPTER 5: ETHNICITY

Ethnic racism is a strong collection of racist policies that result in inequality amongst racialized ethnic groups and is authenticated by racist ideas on racialized ethnic groups. While ethnic antiracism is also a strong collection of antiracist policies that results in equality amongst racialized ethnic groups and is authenticated by antiracist ideas concerning racialized ethnic groups.

When a Black man makes fun of his ethic origin to another Black man, it reawakens the horror of slave trade experience and that can pass as a joke in that regard but not from a White man to a Black man. Ethnic racism's origin can be seen in the slave trade's supply-and-demand market for human produces. Enslavers group their slaves so that they knew those whose ethnicity is pricy and made better slaves. The better slaves were measured as the best Africans. French and Spanish planters felt Congolese and Senegambia made the best slaves respectively. While American's description of the best and most faithful slaves came from the Gold Coast – that's present-day Ghana. Angolans were considered the worst slaves and were classified in the lowest cadre of ethnic racism just above animals. Beneath those ethnic jokes was continental anger; knowing that African chiefs were the ones selling out their people for worthless things.

Africans in the 17th and 18th centuries didn't observe the various ethnic groups surrounding them and acknowledged them as the same race, as Africans. So they didn't think they were selling their own, they felt they sold a different set of the breed to the Europeans. Till the 20th century, it all became clear that selling a fellow African was beyond a savage act.

All through the 1990s, immigrants of color in the U.S. spiked tremendously as a result of the immigration and Nationality Act of 1965, the Refugee Act of 1980, and the Immigration Act of 1990. These bills cheered immigration from conflict inflicted areas, family reunion, and a diversified visa program that increased the number of immigrants from countries outside Europe. The 18th century is known for its upsurge in the immigrants of color. Despite the above, within immigrants of color; silent withdrawal existed that they tried hard to conceal. Further restrictions sprung forth in 1882 – Chinese Restriction Act incorporating Asiatic barred Zone in 1917. In 1921 the Emergency Quota Act and the Immigration Act of 1924 ruthlessly hindered immigrants from Africa and Eastern and Southern Europe and 1965 banned the immigration of Asians.

In 1924 when the numbers of non-native born immigrants spiked in the U.S., senator Jeff Sessions changed the policy. He began executing Trump administration's anti-Arab, anti-Latinx, and anti-Black immigrant policies to purge other nationalities from America and make it White again.

The minute ethnic groups fall under the scrutiny and power of race makers, it becomes racialized. The aim of racializing is to create hierarchies of value. The United States history is an intra-racial ethnic power connection of Anglo-Saxons discriminating against the Irish Catholics and Jews; as Cuban immigrants being fortunate over Mexican immigrants; the model-minority construction that includes East Asians and omits Muslims from South Asia.

Ethnic racism is practiced when a racist idea is expressed about an ethnic group. Ethnic racism just like racism in itself highlights group behavior instead of racial policies.

Attributes of an antiracist;

1. Views national and transnational ethnic groups as equals even in the face of their differences.
2. Challenges racist policies that afflict racialized ethnic groups.
3. To recognize the inequalities between all racialized ethnic groups as a policy delinquent.

Over time, African Americans have repeatedly looked down on African and South American immigrants. Ethnic racism is a strong cankerworm that needs treating and it needs to begin from us then other nationalities will see strong reasons to follow suit. Ethnically racist ideas, similar to all racist ideas, conceal the racist policies exerted against Black natives and immigrants. For Black immigrants to equate their economic standing to that of Black natives and agree that their progress reveals that antiracist Americans are exaggerating racist policies against African Americans, they are indirectly shrinking the chains of racist policy around their wrists.

It is common for Black immigrants to do better than African Americans born into White privilege. This is not far-fetched as these Black immigrants know they have to work double and tripled harder to put food on their table and enjoy the unmerited benefits that individuals in the position of White privilege benefit. Ethnic racism raises a lot of dust, hurt, and confusion suffered by both ethni-related parties.

- **Lessons**
  1. Ethnic racism is a strong collection of racist policies that result in inequality amongst racialized ethnic groups and is authenticated by racist ideas on racialized ethnic groups.
  2. Ethnic antiracism is a strong collection of antiracist policies that results in equality amongst racialized ethnic groups and is authenticated by antiracist ideas concerning racialized ethnic groups.
  3. The minute ethnic groups fall under the scrutiny and power of race makers, it becomes racialized. The aim of racializing is to create hierarchies of value.
- **Issues surrounding the subject matter**
  1. Why is it that African Americans have repeatedly looked down on African and South American immigrants?

  _____

  _____

  _____

  _____

  _____

  2. In what ways have you shown or said that antiracist Americans are exaggerating racist policies against African Americans thereby shrinking the chains of racist policy around your wrists?

  _____

  _____

  _____

  _____

  _____

  _____

- **Goals**

1. What are the ways you can wade off and stop promotin
   ethnic racism?

   _____

   _____

   _____

   _____

   _____

2. What would you do in a situation where a White perso
   throws a racial joke on you? Will you fight, flee, or correct
   Explain what method you will use in this situation.

   _____

   _____

   _____

   _____

   _____

   _____

   _____

   _____

   _____

   _____

   _____

   _____

- **Action steps**
  1. Ethnic racism begins with us and can equally end thus.
- **Checklist**
  1. In ethnic racism, both ethnic groups suffer the result.

CHAPTER 6: BODY

A bodily racist is an individual who thinks that specific racialized bodies as more animalistic and violent than others. On the other hand, a bodily antiracist is one humanizing, individualizing, and deracializing nonviolent and violent behavior.

Today Americans perceive the "Black body" as a threat and harm to their society. They feel the Black body requires more force to dominate than that of the Whites. That explains why the Black body was lynched by thousands, expatriated by tens of thousands, enslaved by millions, and segregated by tens of millions. From a very young age, we have been nurtured not to show off our Black body for fear of being treated inappropriately. The Black body is always watchful as a lot of racist idea of harm and violence is in the thought of a Black body. The Black body is often attacked, manhandled, trampled upon, treated like trash just because it is Black, and black is considered "bad."

The Blackness of the Black body is what seemingly arms us to our teeth that we pose so much threat to the non-Black even without being physically armed. While the Whiteness of the Whites showcase them as the frightened and victimized when they are causing the harm and havoc. The society we live in has forced the people of color to feel that the Black body is a cause and so should stop at nothing to aspire to be White whether by hook or by crook. Blacks comprise 13% of the United States population, yet over 26% were recorded to have been killed by the police in 2015, 24% in 2016, 22% in 2017, and 21% in 2018. Unarmed Black bodies are more likely to be killed as to unarmed White bodies.

Even politically the fear of the Black body showed. Th introduction of the Violent Crime Control and Law Enforcement A in 1993 revealed that the bipartisan group requested $2 billio additional in the act for the drug treatment and $3 billion extra fc violence-prevention programs revealing their fear for the Black bod Republicans tagged those items the criminal's welfare an commanded they be topped back for their votes, Democratic leade yielded – 26 of the 38 voting members of the Congressional Blac Caucus conceded, too. This policy conclusion revealed their duelir consciousness and desire not to lose the prevention fundin completely in rewriting the bill. Though expensive, this crime bi wasn't enough to stop Blacks especially the super-predators.

Paint the most violent situation that occurred or believed t have occurred as a result of young Black children perpetuating crime the truth is that crime bills have never interconnected to crime an more than fear has related to real violence. The Whites are bus fearing the wrong things such as the knelling Arab body praying t Allah, the unarmed Latinx body from Latin America, the burnt Blac looking body, etc. The cops fear the Black bodies; especially racis police officers appear to be more nervous around us.

National Longitudinal Survey of Youth data from 1976 to 198 revealed that young Black males were involved in more violer crimes than young White males. When the researchers did an ir depth comparison using only employed young males of both race: the variances in violent behavior disappeared. That's to say tha when unemployment thrives, crime and violence inevitably increase ue to the increasing jobless enthusiast on the streets. So violence nd crime are not subjected to a particular race or ethnicity.

. typical example is the study sociologist Karen F. Parker underwent nd revealed that when the growth of Black-owned businesses ccurred, there was a massive reduction in Black youth violence etween 1990 and 2000.

the reason for crime is strongly inherent and dependent on the lack body, then the violent-crime rate will be the same regardless f where Black people reside. Segregationists and assimilationist ave called for stricter laws and policies for these super-predators. nstead of making the law tougher, engage these lots, and make the conomy blossom further.

- **Lessons**
    1. A bodily racist is an individual who thinks that specific racialized bodies as more animalistic and violent than others. On the other hand, a bodily antiracist is one humanizing, individualizing, and deracializing nonviolent and violent behavior.
    2. Today Americans perceive the "Black body" as a threat and harm to their society. They feel the Black body requires more force to dominate than that of the Whites.
    3. If the reason for crime is strongly inherent and dependent on the Black body, then the violent-crime rate will be the same regardless of where Blacks are.
- **Issues surrounding the subject matter**
    1. What does it feel like being in a Black body?

_____

_____

_____

_____

_____

2. How has society treated you differently because you ar
   Black?

_____

_____

_____

_____

_____

_____

_____

_____

3. Have you ever experienced severe horror for being Black
   explain here?

_____

_____

_____

_____

_____

_____

_____

_____

- **Goals**
  1. As a Black body how can you remove fear of being harme
  because of your skin color from your consciousness

_____

_____

_____

_____

_____

2. How can you indoctrinate Whites that care to listen that your Black body poses no threat or harm to other races?

_____

_____

_____

_____

_____

1. What role does the family have to play in reducing violence in Black children?

_____

_____

_____

_____

_____

_____

_____

_____

_____

_____

- **Action steps**
    1. The Black body is not a threat to the human race. Abandonment of adequate structures that should have been put in place to enable Black children to be useful to themselves and the community at large is being denied due to White privilege limitations.
- **Checklist**
    1. The Black body is nothing to be ashamed of.

CHAPTER 7: CULTURE

Culture refers to values, beliefs, arts, and principles belonging to people that make them distinct. Cultural racist is an individual who builds a cultural standard and imposes a certain cultural hierarchy between racial groups. On the other hand, cultural antiracists reject cultural standards and equalize cultural variances between racial groups.

In 1996, Ebonics was detested by some Americans. Ebonics had some sort of legitimacy and richness as a language in the wake of cultural antiracism. Ebonics was employed to quicken the understanding and application of the English language to African kids which many found degrading. The African language was seen as improper, broken, and nonstandard. Africans have been discouraged severely to desist from speaking their native dialect that is said to be broken and improper since it isn't the widely accepted English, Spanish, Portuguese, French or Dutch language.

Ebonics grew from the roots of African languages and contemporary English just the way modern English grew from Greek, Latin, and Germanic roots. So why is Ebonics broken English? But English is not broken German or broken Greek? The idea that the African dialect is broken and that of others is fixed are culturally racist. Gunnar Myrda wrote in 1944 on race relations that stood as the "bible" of the civil rights movement. Myrdal's preaching standardized the entire (white American culture and arbitrated the African American culture as distorted and pathologically substandard. The substandard nature of the African culture, therefore, removes us from the cultural hierarchy and only those with standard culture can belong to the cultural hierarchy. The act of culturally categorizing using standards is what brings about cultural racism.

Being antiracist requires you to reject cultural standards and hierarchy categorizing grades of culture. Segregationists believe that racial groups can never match up to their superior cultural standard while assimilationists say racial groups can intentionally make efforts to reach their superior cultural criteria. In 1905 President Theodore Roosevelt implored African Americans to assimilate the superior culture. Alexander Crummell (the stately Episcopalian priest) who discovered the first formal Black intellectual society in 1897, advised fellow Black Americans to assimilate.

Instead of the supposed mainstream to have a large effect on us, our culture – fashion, music, and language started transforming the wider culture. Africans cared less if their language was referred to as substandard or their dress sense pointed out as "wacky". They were comfortable and at peace and that was what mattered. Africans are gifted in making something conventional fresh at all times by always experimenting, elaborating, and being impeccably meticulous – and that unique ability cannot be taken away.

African Americans display outward physical manifestations of European culture – thus making Africans European in culture and language. Bill Cosby said in 2004 that "we are not African". This is based on the fact that it is hard to discover the survival and revival of the real African cultural forms. Surface-sighted evaluation of the Black skin doesn't look inward, behind, and below. That singular act is a faulty and baseless assessment of cultural presence. The aforementioned surface-sighted eyes seek traditional African religions, foods, customs, languages, and fashion to show in the Americans just as it appears in Africa. When it isn't seen, it is automatically assumed that African cultures are overwhelmed by resilient European cultures. This calls for deep cultural structure across the board. That involves including multiculturalism. Referring to a certain group as White or Black or another racial identity—we are racializing that group thereby opening up the portal to cultural racism.

- **Lessons**
  1. Cultural racist is an individual who builds a cultural standard and imposes a certain cultural hierarchy between racial groups.
  2. Cultural antiracist rejects cultural standards and equalizes cultural variances between racial groups.
  3. Being antiracist requires you to reject cultural standards and hierarchy categorizing grades of culture.
- **Issues surrounding the subject matter**
  1. What makes the African language improper and that of the Europeans standard and worldly accepted?

_____
_____
_____
_____
_____
_____
_____
_____

  2. In what ways have you racialized a culture without your knowledge and when you were aware?

_____

_____

_____

_____

_____

- **Goals**
  1. What are your thoughts on Dinesh D'Souza positing that if Blacks can close the civilization gap, the race problem will become insignificant?

  _____

  _____

  _____

  _____

  2. How do you intend to rise above your behaviorally racist insecurity?

  _____

  _____

  _____

  _____

- **Action steps**
  1. There is a call for deep cultural structure across the board.
- **Checklist**
  1. Everyone's culture is distinct and unique; no nationality's culture is more superior to that of others.

CHAPTER 8: BEHAVIOR

A behavioral racist makes people accountable for th
perceived behavior or racial groups and makes the racial group
answerable for the behavior of the individual in question.
behavioral antiracist makes the behavior of a racial group fiction
and that of an individual, tangible.

It is a common habit to critique an individual without basin
the outcome of their mannerism and attributing it to their identifie
race. This is very common in the nonblack; they see our Blacknes
instead of the behavior displayed. So instead of addressing the roc
cause of the problem which is the behavior, they are busy tacklin
the Blackness. The Black skin has since been quite eye-catching an
attractive you can tell so far. It's no wonder the sight of it raises a lc
of dust. The way a Black will represent his race is the same way
White will. So what makes that of a Black man uncomfortable to th
White?

Racial-group behavior is just a figment of the racist
imagination. Personal behaviors can shape the success or failure c
an individual but policies affect the outcome of a large group. Racis
power builds policies that yield racial inequalities. Behavioral racisr
is when an individual is made responsible for the behavior of a racia
group and allow an entire racial group to be blamed for the behavic
of just one individual (as was common in the 1990s), this belie
distorts our perfection of the world we live in. Our success or failur
is not resultant to our racial groups. We are first human beings wit
feelings before we are identified with a racial group. It is high tim
we separate an individual's mannerisms from their race whe

ritiquing the outcome of behavior. This position on cultural racism till exists to date as seen displayed by Trump voters who claim to be onracist but aggressively opposed him in the elections of 2016. Behavioral racism is the wrong metric to gauge, understand, or examine a person's culture. Black behavior is used to judge people's characteristics and attributes.

To believe that there is nothing like racial behavior/irresponsible Black behavior is to be antiracist. Just the way there is no Black gene, there is no scientific fact stating that there are Black behavioral traits. So, enough of the racial behavior BS! Have you seen an empirical study stating that it is natural for Black people to be louder, nicer, angrier, lazier, funnier, more immoral, less punctual, very religious, more dependent, etc? The way to go is to separate the notion of a people's culture from the idea of their behavior. Culture signifies a group's tradition shared by a specific racial group but not shared amongst all individuals in that racial group or between all racial groups.

Our behavior defines our intrinsic human traits and potential. Racist behaviorists believe that a people's race largely defines how they behave. It was also exemplified from the slavery and freedom experience, positing that the horror of slavery and the struggle for freedom was a result of the mediocre Black behavior. Once the mind holds something behaviorally wrong within a racial group, then the mind won't be antiracist and vice versa. A racist mind can never be free; to be antiracist is to be the following;

1. To think nothing is wrong or right behaviorally within a racial group.

1. To think nothing is behaviorally inferior or superior within racial group.
2. To deracialize behavior.
3. To take out tattooed stereotypes from racialized bodies.

- **Lessons**
  1. A behavioral racist makes people accountable for th perceived behavior or racial groups and makes the racia groups answerable for the behavior of the individual i question.
  2. A behavioral antiracist makes the behavior of a racia group fictional and that of an individual, tangible.
  3. There is yet to be an empirical study stating that a person' behavior is a result of where they come from.
- **Issues surrounding the subject matter**
  1. Why do you think the Black skin makes nonblac uncomfortable?

  _____

  _____

  _____

  _____

  2. Is it possible to separate a people's culture from thei behavior and how can one go about that?

  _____

  _____

  _____

  _____

  _____

  _____

- **Goals**
  1. How do you think you can separate a people's culture from their behavior?

  _____

  _____

  _____

  _____

  _____

  _____

  _____

  2. Are you a behavioral racist or antiracist and what are your attributes based on your chosen position?

  _____

  _____

  _____

  _____

  _____

  _____

  _____

  _____

  _____

  _____

  _____

- **Action steps**
  1. To believe that there is nothing like racial behavior/irresponsible Black behavior is to be antiracist.
- **Checklist**
  1. Behavior is a thing humans do, not races do.

CHAPTER 9: COLOR

Colorism is a strong collection of racist policies that bring about inequities among those identified as White people and Black people, sustained by racist ideas about Whites and Blacks. Color antiracism is equally a powerful assemblage of antiracist policies that bring about equities among White people and Black people, sustained by antiracist ideas about Whites and Blacks.

The widely accepted racial appearance is the lightened skin, the straighter hair, thinner nose, semi-thick lips, lighter eyes, and semi-thick buttocks. This is the standard way any human should look – the modern form of colorism; a term invented by novelist Alice Walker in 1983. Most antiracists look up to another race and desire to have what they have. The feeling of dissatisfaction is the dueling consciousness here. This post-racial beauty characteristic hides colorism and covers it in euphemism. Colorism is another method of racism. Getting to understand racism requires recognizing the fact that Light and Dark people come from two different racial groups formed by their various histories. The distinct physical features they both have are unique to them based on race.

Some activists project that the Light people are the biracial key to racial coherence, an epitome of a post-racial future. Colorism is all forms of inequality at play. Colorist justifies inequalities with ideas that are racist and claims that the inequality amongst Dark people and White people is not as a result of the racist policies but because something fundamental is wrong with the racial group. Colorist projects an assimilationist idea that encourages adjustment or transformation into the White body.

Here is what an antiracist will do in this situation;

1. Pay attention to the color lines as much as racial lines, being aware that color lines are especially harmful to Dark people.
2. Not reversing the beauty standard.
3. Eradicate any beauty standard centered on the skin and eye color, facial and bodily features, and hair texture shared by groups.
4. Diversify our criteria of beauty like our standards of culture or astuteness.
5. See beauty equally in all skin colors, kinky and straight hair, light and dark eyes, and broad and thin noses.
6. Build and dwell in a beauty culture that emphasizes instead of wiping out our natural beauty.

When a Dark African American student attains an academic stride, he is remembered as a Light-skinned even with his visible Dark skin. The Light skin receives higher wages, and their daughters get higher-quality parenting. The son with the Dark skin receives higher-quality parenting than the Dark daughters and even Light skin sons.

Lighter skin tone is an indication of beauty for most Black women. They aspire to have lighter skin as they perceive that is the only way they can truly be beautiful. Skin tone heightens self-esteem levels within Black women and it is on the increase by the day. Dark-skinned African Americans receive very harsh prison sentences and spend more time behind bars. Light skinned women are perceived to be more intelligent, nicer, gentler, and more beautiful than Dark women.

But the struggle isn't entirely one-sided, the whites also hav struggles to contend with as regards their color. The whites get i wrong occasionally as they are trying to integrate with dark peopl and feel rejected. The Whites try to prove their Blackness to peopl of color as if the Blacks are the judge of the standards of Blackness The harsh irony is that these same Blacks that the Whites struggle t integrate with are aspiring to live up to the standard of Whiteness.

Ever heard of – the one-drop rule? It states that a single drop of th Black blood makes one Black to discourage one from pure Whitenes (used by Whites). On the other hand, Dark people use the two-dro rule which says – two drops of White blood makes one less Black an then the three-drop rule says —three drops of the Black blood make one too Dark. But these rules are just a mirage because no racia group is totally pure. Nevertheless, slaveholder's philosophy state that the Whiter the skin is, the more superior it is. No wonder the are given skilled positions while the Blacks are given physica demanding jobs.

In 1865 after the emancipation freed the Blacks from captivity members of the White community built higher walls to keep out th Blacks; and the same was carried out by the Light people to maintai Light privileges. This made them richer than Dark people after slaver and that put them on a higher pedestal as they had good-paying job and education. Towards the end of the 19th century a lot of peopl had "Blue Vein" in the society (all the more to keep the Dark peopl out). During these times, to lay with a Black is the most diabolic an debilitating of all sins.

Dating to contemporary times, skin color inequality still glooms. To attain certain high standards in society, you have to physically appear in widely approved ways. This is applicable in the movie industry, in sport, at our place of work, in our neighborhood, and even as you walk on the streets. No wonder the sale of bleaching cream is still on the rise. Foreign companies producing these products are cashing out in millions. Nigeria ranks the highest purchasers of skin lighteners with 70 percent, 59 percent in Togo, 35 percent in South Africa, and 40 percent in China, Malaysia, South Korea, and the Philippines. The Whites also have their skin-care addiction which is to get a post-racial skin tone achieved by "tanning."

- **Lessons**

    1. People of Dark skin rarely protest policies that benefit an individual with Light skin, a "skin color paradox," – a term coined by political scientists Jennifer L. Hochschild and Vesla Weaver.
    2. Skin tone heightens self-esteem levels within Black women and it is on the increase by the day.
    3. To attain certain high standards in society, you have to physically appear in widely approved ways.
    4. Some activists project that the Light people are the biracial key to racial coherence, an epitome of a post-racial future. But this is just their opinion.

- **Issues surrounding the subject matter**
    1. In what ways have you tried to show your Blackness to a person of Dark skin and you were shunned or rejected and how did you handle that rejection?

_____

_____

_____

_____

_____

_____

_____

_____

2. What is your honest opinion of the Dark skin and are you of the opinion that there exists a more superior skin or that all skin tone is equal?

_____

_____

_____

_____

- **Goals**
  1. In what ways can you feel comfortable in your skin as a Black person?

_____

_____

_____

_____

_____

_____

_____

_____

2. How can Dark people avoid taking too much pride in their Black skin thereby inverting the color hierarchy?

_____

_____

_____

_____

_____

3. How can you correct the notion by a colorist saying that the inequality amongst Dark people and White people is not as a result of the racist policies, but because something fundamental is wrong with the racial group?

_____

_____

_____

_____

_____

_____

_____

_____

_____

- **Action steps**
  1. Nothing is wrong with your racial group because a colorist said so. Colorism is meant to cause discord amongst a racial group so that they think that they have a problem, whereas it is the policy that binds them that needs amending.
- **Checklist**
  1. Colorism is all forms of inequality at play.

CHAPTER 10: WHITE

An anti-white racist is an individual that categorizes people c European origin as culturally, biologically, or behaviorally inferior c mixing the entire race of White people with racist power.

In the 2000 election, the income and educational levels or ruthles ballot designs were hard to expatiate as it concerned racial inequit – according to New York Times statistical analysis. This was clear cu racism at play, but did anyone have the nerve to counter it? Blac had enough votes to win but we were sent home and some other had their votes destroyed. Then some uninformed racists will com up to blame Blacks – the victimized race for their victimization. A antiracist is courageous. Courage is not the nonexistence of fear bu the strength and audacity to do what is right in the face of it.

History has a lot of documents dating back and even in recent time of how the Black race was victimized and this only helps to bree more and more hatred amongst the Blacks and Whites. Imagin segregating human beings using colors of grade them – there is th White race, the Yellow race, the Brown race, and the Black race. Th Blacks are presumed to live in the bushes and caves in Africa with n form of civilization until a savior came to rescue them. When slaver and colonialism ended, Africans were still far from their civilizatio as that of White people. Then Blacks indulged in criminal acts an ended up being segregated, lynched, and mass-imprisonment b officers in developed nations of the world. The developing Blac countries were spitted with corruption, lack of skill, ethnic strife unstable and poor.

Ibram X. Kendi explained Elijah Muhammad's White degrading an horrific creation story and other followers walked in his footstep such as Malcolm X who faced similar incarceration and torture jus or propagating his religion and beliefs. Blacks can also be racist towards White people; a typical example is the famous NOI's White-evil idea. This situation was a typical case of race classification ased on biological, cultural, or behavioral inferiority and blaming their race as a result. That is not to say that the Whites didn't enslave, impoverish, massacre and colonized millions of indigenous people of color – which their economy grew fat on. There is no such thing as White genes.

An antiracist will do the following;

1. Never mistake antiracist hate of White racism for that of racist hate of White people.
2. Never mix racist people with White people because there are antiracist Whites and racist non-Whites.
3. See regular White people as the common victimizers of people of color and victims of racist power.

The common White people benefit from racist policies, although not as much as they would have from an equitable society where a White voter is powerful and rich enough to decide elections and shape policy. Ideas not centered on White lives are considered racist. That why the Whites respond to the "Black Lives Matter" with "All Lives Matter" and "Blue Lives Matter." Anti-white racism is the "hate" that "hate" created endearing to the victims of White racism. But still, racist power flourishes on anti-White racist ideas and hate even fuels its power the more. This simply tells us that to hate a Black person is to automatically hate a White person.

- **Lessons**
  1. An anti-white racist is an individual that categorizes peopl of European origin as culturally, biologically, c behaviorally inferior or mixing the entire race of Whit people with racist power.
  2. There is no such thing as White genes.
  3. Blacks can also be racist towards White people; a typica example is the famous NOI's White-devil idea.
- **Issues surrounding the subject matter**
  1. Why do you think hate exists amongst the Whites and th Blacks?

  _____

  _____

  _____

  _____

  _____

  2. Can there actually be a time when all racial groups ca coexist in peace and harmony?

  _____

  _____

  _____

  _____

  _____

- **Goals**
  1. As an antiracist how can you indoctrinate an anti-whit racist based on the sort of idea they have about racis power?

  _____

  _____

  _____

_____

_____

_____

_____

_____

_____

_____

2. In what ways have you been racist to a White as a Black and what would you have done better based on the knowledge you have now?

_____

_____

_____

_____

_____

_____

_____

_____

- **Action steps**

    1. Make a list of ways you intend to never mix up antiracist hate of White racism for that of racist hate of White people.

- **Checklist**

    1. Racial hate only makes matters worse; erase hate and a lot of things will be sorted.

CHAPTER 11: BLACK

The powerless defense is a situation that is built on deceit, concealment, disempowerment on racist idea that Black people cannot be racist since Black people don't have power.

White racists have done a good job at schooling us on how to generalize the personal characteristics we see in a certain Black person. We have learned not to see and treat fellow Blacks as individuals, but as a group identified as niggers with their hierarchy. Imagine that we get upset when Whites call us niggers when we gave them every reason to.

But here is what the Blacks did and didn't do respectfully;

We racialized the bad behavior and attached loudness, laziness and criminality to niggers, like White racists, as Black racists	We didn't place loud, lazy and criminal Black people in a multicultural group of similar people

We identified ourselves as nonracists just like the White racists. The dueling consciousness here reveals how the Blacks distinguish themselves from niggers just like the Whites. The Blacks experience shame and pride in their Black excellence as they disassociate from niggers. They are perceived as criminals, this is a show of Black on Black crime. Blacks are fond of turning on themselves when they need to make a positive mark in the society. A typical example occurred is Obama's era when more than 60 percent of Black people moved over to join the White majority that says that racism isn't the reason for racial inequalities. This scenario is just one out of many. For every time you see something wrong with the Black race, you as a Black man is separating yourself from them and all they represent lacks are not totally powerless as posited. Black people can be racist o matter the limited amount of power ascribed. History has ecorded that the history of Black racism began in 1526 in Africa. acist ideas cage people and limit their power to resist dominance. ust the way Black believes the Whites have all the power in the vorld to do as they please. This notion a Black segregationist will ght but a Black assimilationist will worship, defend, and strive to be ke.

- **Lessons**
  1. The powerless defense is a situation that is built on deceit, concealment, disempowerment on racist idea that Black people cannot be racist since Black people don't have power.
  2. Black people can be racist no matter the limited amount of power ascribed.
- **Issues surrounding the subject matter**
  1. The saying "Black people can't be racist" is based on fallacy or truth, and what are the reasons for your response?

  _____

  _____

  _____

  _____

  _____

  2. In what ways can you use your power for positive racial gains?

  _____

  _____

  _____

  _____

_____

_____

_____

_____

_____

- **Goals**
  1. Blacks have power although seemingly limited but can sti
     pull some weight. In what ways can you end Black on Blac
     racism as an individual and collectively as a racial group?

     _____

     _____

     _____

     _____

     _____

  2. How can one attain a single consciousness of antiracism?

     _____

     _____

     _____

     _____

     _____

- **Action steps**
  1. Separation from our indigenous racial group can b
     expunged if we tackle it from the root and that is by callin
     for a review of the racial policies that affect us all.
- **Checklist**
  1. With great power comes far greater responsibility. Use th
     amount of power you have as a desired nationality t
     make a change racially.

CHAPTER 12: CLASS

, class racist is one who racializes class by supporting policies of acial capitalism against race-classes and justifies them by imploring acist ideas as it concerns those race-classes. While an antiracist nticapitalist is one who opposes racial capitalism.

, policy that takes advantage of poor people to enrich themselves he more is elitist. A policy that rides on the coat-tails of Black poor eople is doing so from an elitist and racist policy angle – that is class acism. An antiracist equalizes race-classes and not segregates. An ntiracist blames the pathological nature of the political and conomic conditions and not the people in poor Black eighborhoods. An antiracist hinges the economic differences mongst the equal races-classes in policies and not people. Class acism is prevalent amongst White American who look down on ellow Whites called "White trash" and the Black American who lespises fellow poor Black and refer to them as "niggers." Concepts f "White trash" and "ghetto Blacks" are very obvious ideologies of :lass racism.

f an elite belonging to race-class judges the poor race-classes based n their cultural and behavioral standards automatically makes the oor race-classes seem inferior. The creators of the norms created he hierarchy and place their race-class at the topmost of the iierarchy. In 1959 anthropologist Oscar Lewis coined the term 'culture of poverty" which argues that poor children color were ntentionally raised on conducts that hindered them from breaking out from the jinx of poverty. This notion alone has spread poverty across generations. He further came up with an elitist idea that poor behaviors keep poor people poor. Kenneth Clark didn't agree with Lewis, he is of the opinion that racism, discrimination, defeat, oppression-inferiority, slavery, and segregation are the reason fo repeated phases of poverty amongst the people of color. Th absence of welfare made poor people poorer. The feeling o hopelessness and defeat is enough to leave poor Black unmotivated.

Black elitism began to look down on their poor fellows (niggers) th same way the White elitist degradingly looks down on Blacks. All th was due to their raised wages and affluence. During these time ghetto became more of an adjective culturally and as a noun when concerned the people. Black on Black crimes heightened and quantifiable number of racist ideas flooded the Black society.

Prince Henry introduced capitalism and racism when he introduce slavery. Even in 2017, the rate of Black poverty was 20 percent whic is almost twice as high as that of the White unemployment rate fo fifty years now. A 2020 forecast has it that a White home is expecte to have eighty-sixed times more affluence than the Black household This forecast will manifest as long as the already rich ones kee eating off the little gains of the poor. This large disparity worsen because of racist housing policies, tax policies promoting the rich an mass imprisonment continue unflinchingly.

Sociologists posit that ascribing inequities exclusively to capitalism i as damaged as assigning them solely to racism. Also being positiv that these inequities will be eradicated by removing capitalism is a defective as trusting these inequalities will be eradicated b abolishing racism. To eliminate class racism, antiracist policies nee anti-capitalist policies. The same goes for anticapitalism; as it canno take out class racism minus of antiracism.

U.S. senator Elizabeth Warren gives a different view of capitalism. She made us know that when there is no level playing field in the markets, all the wealth ends up in the pocket a very few. Capitalism has never been theft, and she suggested a series of regulations and reforms that her conformist opponents call "anti-capitalist." Nevertheless, the wealth extraction exists till date, through foreign organizations owning key natural resources and returning to their homelands to develop it.

- **Lessons**
  1. A class racist is one who racializes class by supporting policies of racial capitalism against race-classes and justifies them by imploring racist ideas as it concerns those race-classes.
  2. An antiracist anticapitalist is one who opposes racial capitalism.
- **Issues surrounding the subject matter**
  1. In what ways have you snitched on your fellow Black man to favor the opposition, just to remain in the steady hierarchy of the food chain?

  _____

  _____

  _____

  _____

  _____

  2. Explain in detail your experience with Black on Black racism, whether personally or as a witness to one?

  _____

  _____

  _____

_____

_____

- **Goals**
  1. What role does White privilege play in Black on Black racism?

  _____

  _____

  _____

  _____

  _____

  2. Capitalism and racism coexist together, what do you think is the possible solution to end this racial class classification?

  _____

  _____

  _____

  _____

  _____

- **Action steps**
  1. Map out a constructive plan to erase racism, discrimination, defeat, oppression-inferiority, slavery, and segregation as the reasons for repeated phases of poverty amongst the people of color.
- **Checklist**
  1. If you love capitalism then you love racism. These destructive twins walk together.

CHAPTER 13: SPACE

Space racism refers to the great collection of racist policies leading to resource inequality amongst racialized spaces or the eradication of specific racialized spaces that are authenticated by racist ideas about racialized spaces. On the other hand, space antiracism is the powerful grouping of antiracist policies that ushers equality amongst united and endangered racialized spaces that are validated by antiracist ideas about racialized spaces.

The African space is the Black space because it is ruled by Black bodies, Black minds, Black cultures, and histories. In 1980, Molefi Kete Asante published the seminal work Afrocentricity that criticized the assimilationist ideas and necessitated for Afrocentric Black people. She advised that in situations where you can't be objective, just tell the whole truth. It is much better. The racist Whites bothered about their White space in a Black dominated space and wondered why Blacks will be worried about their own space in a White space.

Just like Kenneth Clark said in 1960– the symbol of Harlem's "dark ghetto." He said that juvenile delinquency and widespread violence were the constant attributes existent in various forms of racialized spaces and weren't a phenomenon set aside for only the people of color. The saying that – "Black neighborhood is dangerous" is the most hazardous racist idea and it is equally robustly misleading. The stigmatization meted out on the Black race didn't start today; it's been a long time coming. The notion racist Americans have that nothing good ever comes from Blacks has been in existence for many decades.

As racist power racializes individuals, the same racist power racializes space. When you free yourself from the space racism that lifts, stabilizes and deracializes elite, White spaces as you keep practicing the opposite of Black spacing, you will discover good and bad, violence and non-violence in all spaces regardless of the social class you belong to; nor your Blackness or non-Blackness. Resources have been a definitive factor for space, resources the adjoined twins apportion. Matching spaces across race-classes is the same as bringing fighters with uneven weight groups to compete which are unfair sport-wise. Comparisons are worthy when they are between components within similar ranges and not exact opposites. Comparing poor Blacks to poor Whites in their respective neighborhoods is justifiable and not when the same components are compared with the very rich Whites. If the comparison isn't fair then it's a deliberate slaughter.

This comparison affects Blacks financially, physically, and socially This makes Blacks struggle for everything in life, banks are less likely to give Blacks loans for their businesses no matter how credible they prove to be. The origin of space racism has Thomas Jefferson to thank. He proposed a solution to the "Negro challenge" in other to emancipate and civilize the Black race. When Negros were given the leverage to return to their homeland and spread the seeds of civilization, a quantifiable number refused going back to barbarism and ignorance, thus they remained in the land of their suffrage. In 1885 Segregationists came up with tactics to fade out the line between separation and segregation by showcasing their policies built on equal accommodations for every race but separately. But the segregation persisted in every facet of the society.

Integrationists clamored for the integration of the Whites and Blacks in schools, places of work, religious gatherings, housing, etc. They believe that assimilation will favor all race-classes in the long run. The logical resolve of the integrationist strategy means the race will be represented in different and unequal proportions across the U.S. space in percentages as stated in the national population. By now I am sure you can tell that this strategy will only further empower Whites and give them control to head every facet of the community due to their high population percentage.

Antiracist calls for equal access to all communal accommodations assimilated White spaces, integrated Black spaces, combined Middle Eastern spaces, assimilated Latinx spaces, and integrated Native spaces. An antiracist infuses desegregation with a form of integration and racial solidarity – wading off stumbling blocks of racialized spaces. An antiracist backs the deliberate integration of bodies involved by cultural disparity but with a shared humanity. An antiracist integrates resources justly and challenges racist policies that make resource injustice. An antiracist employs racial solidarity to openly identify, support, and protect integrated racial spaces.

- **Lessons**

    1. Space racism refers to the great collection of racist policies leading to resource inequality amongst racialized spaces or the eradication of specific racialized spaces that are authenticated by racist ideas about racialized spaces.
    2. Space antiracism is the powerful grouping of antiracist policies that ushers equality amongst united and

endangered racialized spaces that are validated by antiracist ideas about racialized spaces.

- **Issues surrounding the subject matter**

    1. Can racial space ever be even?

    _____

    _____

    _____

    _____

    _____

    2. How does the racial policy have a role to play in racial spacing?

    _____

    _____

    _____

    _____

    _____

- **Goals**

    1. As an antiracist, how can you use racial solidarity to openly identify, support, and protect integrated racial spaces?

    _____

    _____

    _____

    _____

    _____

    2. As an antiracist, how can you infuse desegregation with a system of integration and racial solidarity in a racial space

_____

_____

_____

_____

_____

_____

_____

3. In what ways has racial spacing affected you financially, economically, and physically and what do you think can be done to suppress this menace?

_____

_____

_____

_____

_____

_____

- **Action steps**

  1. When you cannot be objective; just tell the whole truth.
- **Checklist**

  1. The antiracist strategy is far from the integrationist notion that says Black spaces might never be equal to White spaces, which considers Black spaces have a harmful effect on Whites.

CHAPTER 14: GENDER

Gender racism is one prodigious grouping of racist policies that lead to inequality amongst race-genders and can be demonstrated b racist ideas on race-genders. Gender antiracism is the exact opposit of the above definition. It is an exceptional grouping of antiracis strategies leading to equality amongst race-genders and can b corroborated by antiracist ideas on race-genders.

In 1965, Daniel Patrick Moynihan; President Johnson's assistan secretary of labor wrote a government report which stated tha almost one-fourth of Black families are headed by women. This wa two times the rate for White families which was a great concern. H claimed that the Black community is now shoved into a matriarcha construct which is a yoke on the Male. This brought about the nee to call for national action on the employment of the Black male who has been made powerless through discrimination and matriarcha Black women. Moynihan's report was met with disastrou reverberations.

Black husbands and White social scientists clamored for submissior from Black women to elevate the race. Black women were implore to allow their Black husband to be the head indeed in their homes In 1976 sociologist Charles Herbert Stember's book on "Sexua Racism: The Emotional Barrier to an Integrated Society" maintaine that the Black male was the main target of racism and that it wa glaring. He noticed that racial sexual rejection was a notable facto amongst the Whites and Blacks. The White man is envious of the Black man's sexual prowess which seems like a gift for a Black man – that was the key issue.

In the 1970s and 1980s, the growing rate of single-parent households was a cause for concern. There were certain factors responsible for this, such as;

1. Bad parenting
2. Abusive Black father
3. Getting a second source of income to cater for the child
4. Incarcerated or dead

In 1994, the percentage of Black children born into single-parent homes got to 68 percent. Political scientist; Charles Murray blamed it all on the poor "welfare system." Others blamed sexual frivolity, a disgraceful disdain for the prospects present in the 1960s activism, pathologizing poverty, and detach from the premarital asceticism of Christ.

The nineteen-seventies ushered in the Black feminist movement initiated in the wake of racial sexism. Black feminists refuted the Black patriarchal idea that the core activist role of a Black woman is to be submissive to her husband and produce more Black babies for the "Black nation." Feminist groups came together to fight sexism in Black spaces and racism in women's spaces. Maria Stewart (America's first feminist), Sojourner Truth, Ida B. Wells, Frances Harper, Anna Julia Cooper, Frances Beal, Nikki Giovanni, Alice Walker, and Audre Lorde all fought justly for Black women from 1830-1970 to end the projection of Black women as victims of the double jeopardy – racism, and sexism (symbols of inequality).

Gender racism has put Black women to strive so much to get what they deserve. Black women who are more qualified than their White counterparts are given degrading jobs while the less qualified Whites head over them. The Whites also earn so much more than the more qualified Black woman, these factors further widen the poverty gap for the Black woman. The Black woman is three to four times more likely to die from pregnancy based challenges than White women. The Black woman is also likely to be losing her child and get incarcerated twice as probable as the White woman.

White women and Black male resistance to Black have been self-destructive, preventing protesters from accepting our specific oppression. The meeting point of racism and sexism, in some cases, subjugates men of color. Black men reinforce oppressive tropes by reinforcing certain sexist ideas. A racist sees the Black man as a weakling and inferior while a sexist concept of a real man is a strong man.

When the innocent Black man encounters gender racism, he is transformed into a dreaded criminal and the White female criminal into Casey Anthony (the White woman a Florida jury acquitted in 2011, for killing her three-year-old child). Black men rot in jail for unjust convictions while White women get away with murder.

The intersectional theory allows the whole of humanity to comprehend the intersectional oppression of their individualities.

- **Lessons**

    1. Gender racism exposes one to colorism, ethnocentrism, sexism, transphobia and homophobia.

2. Gender racism is one prodigious grouping of racist policies that leads to inequality amongst race-genders and can be demonstrated by racist ideas on race-genders.
3. Gender antiracism is an exceptional grouping of antiracist strategies leading to equality amongst race-genders and can be corroborated by antiracist ideas on race-genders.

- **Issues surrounding the subject matter**

1. What are your experiences with gender racism and did it make or mar you?

_____

_____

_____

_____

_____

_____

_____

_____

_____

_____

_____

- **Goals**
    1. How can gender racism be abolished?

_____

_____

_____

_____

_____

_____

_____

_____

_____

2. What policies can be put in place to checkmate gender
   racism on all levels?

_____

_____

_____

_____

_____

_____

_____

_____

_____

- **Action steps**

  1. Identify all your forms of racism and make feasible plan
     to get rid of them. It will not be easy as you have had i
     inside of you for a long time, let the process be natural.

- **Checklist**

  1. When humanity gets serious about Black women'
     freedom, then humanity has become serious about th
     freedom of the whole of humanity.

CHAPTER 15: SEXUALITY

Queer racism is a strong collection of racist policies leading to inequity amongst race-sexualities that can be substantiated by racist ideas as regards race-sexualities. While queer antiracism is the phenomenal gathering of antiracist policies leading to equity amongst race-sexualities for authentication by antiracist ideas on race-sexualities.

Racist power differentiates race-sexualities, racial groups at the juncture of race and sexuality. There are other forms of sexuality asides conventional ones such as homosexuals and heterosexuals. Any homophobic construct will bring about inequalities among homosexuals and heterosexuals. Queer racism is all out to dish inequalities amongst race-sexualities. The segregation and oppression from the system for Black individuals with special sexuality are skin deep. They live in poverty compared to their White counterparts, especially the Black male same-sex couples.

A racist idea on Black people says that Blacks are more hyperactively sexual than the Whites. A homophobic idea proposes that queer people are more hyperactively sexual than heterosexuals traverse to create the queer racism of the most hypersexual race-sexuality, "the Black queer" – the unconventional conspicuous clitoris particular in colored women.

Gender is authentic. The way various gender acts is not hinged on their biology. Genuinely, Men can be women and women can in turn be men thereby daring the society's gender conventions.

Queer antiracism is striving to destroy inequalities within race sexualities and equate all the race-sexualities. Every race-sexuality is unique. All Black Lives Matter including the vulnerable transgender woman and man of color. Enough of the violence and transphobia. As an antiracist, understand the privileges of each gender, cisgender, masculinity, heterosexuality, of their intersections. See racism, homophobia, and queer racism as the problem/abnormality in the situation and not the people nor the queer space. Be their ally, listen to them, learn from them, and follow their equalizing ideas, support their equalizing policy campaigns to attain equal opportunity to live their sexuality.

- **Lessons**

    1. Queer racism is a strong collection of racist policies leading to inequity amongst race-sexualities that can be substantiated by racist ideas as regards race-sexualities.
    2. Queer antiracism is the phenomenal gathering of antiracist policies leading to equity amongst race sexualities for authentication by antiracist ideas on race sexualities.
    3. Every race-sexuality is unique.

- **Issues surrounding the subject matter**

    1. In what ways can you be a successful gender and queer antiracist?

    _____

    _____

    _____

    _____

_____

_____

_____

_____

_____

_____

2. Explain why everything about race is tied to lay down policies that predominantly cause so much harm to other racial groups?

_____

_____

_____

_____

_____

_____

_____

_____

_____

- **Goals**

  1. In what ways has your sexuality been threatened, how did you go about it and what would you have done differently?

  _____

  _____

  _____

  _____

  _____

  _____

_____

_____

_____

_____

2. Map out the modus operandi you intend to begin helping to protect and shield vulnerable homosexuals an heterosexuals henceforth?

_____

_____

_____

_____

_____

_____

_____

_____

_____

_____

_____

- **Action steps**

  1. Being an ally is a starting point for individuals of specia sexualities.

- **Checklist**

  1. You can't be antiracist and homophobic at the same time

CHAPTER 16: FAILURE

An activist is someone with a known record of power and policy iterations.

The racial history of failure is tied to failed solutions and policies. The failed solutions and policies are due to failed racial principles. There are several wrong notions of race we need to debunk before we go further.

1. Race as a social construct, not a power construct!
2. Race's racial history as a singular match of racial progress and not a combat of antiracist and racist progress!
3. Race's problem being ingrained in ignorance and hatred and not powerful selfish interest!

All of the above sums up to solutions guaranteed to fail. When we say we are not racist but racially progressive, that only screams racist aloud the more. The Black community impressed the need for all Blacks to always represent the race well at all times. This eliminates any room for imperfections. Blacks have been made to appear perfect in the presence of Whites and the judges being the Blacks scoring if their fellow Blacks represented the race well.

The uplift suasion has attracted a lot of critiques. Critiques evaluating White protesters summoning up uplift suasion, assumptions that poor Black people's behavior is the reason for White racist ideas thereby making racist ideas about Black mannerism valid, evaluating the vindication of White people by a White judge to take away the responsibility of riding themselves off of racist ideas, Black people ditching being responsible for altering racist policy by thinking they are uplifting the race by uplifting themselves, the close impossibility of perfectly executing uplift suasion as Black people are human imperfect an can never do anything orderly/right. Every time a Black person is oppressed by racist policy the judge commands that the uplift themselves and say nothing about the demeaning policy.

An antiracist is comfortable in their imperfections as no one is truly perfect except God. In the long run, uplift suasion failed miserably in the fight to end slavery in the era of King Cotton. Moral and educational suasion concentrates on coaxing White people, or engaging their moral conscience from fear and their rational mind through education. Gunnar Myrdal called for Black people to focus on amassing power instead of persuading White people as the white know what they are doing.

The antiracist powers within help to see racism in the mirror of the past and present, observe antiracism in the mirror of the future, see racial groups equally, see the abnormality in the world of racial inequity, see the power to resist and outdo racist power and policy

There are a lot of impartial laws and racist policies to be contended with as already outlined from the start of this book. Organizing and protesting are much harder and more impactful than mobilizing and demonstrating. But it is hard to create that environment because racist power has laid down laws that illegalize most protest threats. Seizing power is far tedious than protesting power and demonstrating its excesses.

- **Lessons**

1. An activist is someone with a known record of power and policy alterations.
2. The racial history of failure is tied to failed solutions and policies.
- **Issues surrounding the subject matter**
  1. In your opinion does political, economic, or cultural self-interest motivates racist policymakers and not hateful immorality and ignorance and why?

  _____
  _____
  _____
  _____
  _____
  _____

  2. How can you discover your antiracist power within?

  _____
  _____
  _____
  _____

- **Goals**
  1. How can racism be truly defeated?

  _____
  _____
  _____
  _____
  _____

  2. How can you persuade Whites alongside the racist policymakers to alter the cruel policies that endanger the people of color?

_____

_____

_____

_____

_____

_____

_____

_____

_____

_____

3. What if racist policymakers know about the harmful outcomes of their policies, will that help to alleviate the racial oppression faced by the Blacks?

_____

_____

_____

_____

_____

- **Action steps**
  1. Time and time again the strategies and policies to help end racism keep failing, what is the missing piece you think we are all leaving out? It's time to return to the drawing board.
- **Checklist**
  1. Race is a powerful construct.

CHAPTER 17: SUCCESS

1 trying to illustrate racism and liken it to disease is faulty because it
s not deep and ground-breaking enough to stand as a claim. It has
een observed that the perception anyone takes as to what racism
neans largely depends on their ideology and self-identity. Telling an
ntiracist to alter their perception of racism is as wrecking and
listurbing as telling a racist to change their notions on race as well.
s an antiracist is rigid in their views on racism, the same applies to
nost racist on their views on racism.

orrowing the formulae coined in 1967 by Black Power activist
wame Toure as well as political scientist Charles Hamilton in Black
ower: The Politics of Liberation in America. It says that racism is
lisplayed overtly and covertly; meaning it is carried out openly and
iidden but carried out individually and institutionally. This practice
f racism is effective when perpetrated by individual Whites against
ndividual Blacks and by the entire White community against the
Black community. Whether racism is practiced individually or as an
nstitution on the supposed minors, it is racism, very degrading,
lehumanizing, and increases suicidal instincts in its sufferers.

ndividuals acting out racism can be on one confrontation in various
acets; religious organizations, school, place of work, in the
ieighborhood, on the street, in the mall, etc. Racism is practiced
nstitutionally through segregated policies that are intentionally
oined to make individuals of non-White privilege toil, suffer, and go
hrough unimaginable situations just to gain the unmerited benefits
vasted by White privilege holders. Racism makes Whites gain more
han Blacks in all ramifications. Whether practiced covertly or

overtly, racism supports and promotes racial inequalities. Th
intention of covering racism is so that you will find it hard to identi
racist acts and focus your aggression on non-existent things in socie
to blame for the inequality.

Racist acts are overt if you as an antiracist can identify the raci
policy inherent in racial inequality. From the onset, the U.S. has bee
a racist nation due to its policymakers and policies. For policymake
to change their policies, their thinking has to be altered to mak
effective changes in the policy. Racism can be cured even with i
terminal qualities. The toxicity can be cured, the demeaning word
can be withdrawn, the slavery notion can be terminated, th
dehumanizing identifications can stop and the animalist sexu
conception erased for good.

Attributes of a successful antiracist;

1. Stop saying the "I am not racist" defense.
2. Admit the description of racist ascribed to you.
3. Be truthful about the racist ideas you support and express.
4. Own the source of your racial information acquisition.
5. Own up to your definition of antiracism.
6. Be proud of your antiracist power struggles and policies i
   your space.
7. Making public donations of your time and resources to th
   propagation of antiracist policies by funding antiraci
   policymakers and protests for fundamental racial changes.
8. Being an antiracist in the face of other racial bigotries.
9. Be open about your struggles with antiracist ideas.
10. Not easily fooled into generalizing individual negativity.

11. Not fooled into believing misleading statistics blaming people for racial inequality.

- **Lessons**
    1. Our ideology and self-identity play a huge role in understanding what racism means.
    2. Turning from a racist to an antiracist is as difficult as changing from an antiracist to a racist, the struggle is real.
    3. Whether racism is practiced individually or as an institution on the supposed minors, it is racism, very degrading, dehumanizing, and increases suicidal instincts in its sufferers.
- **Issues surrounding the subject matter**
    1. What are your concerns about the covert form of racism?

_____

_____

_____

_____

_____

_____

_____

_____

_____

- **Goals**
    1. Would you join Boyce Watkins to describe racism as a disease and why would you or wouldn't?

_____

_____

_____

2. What is racism to you and do you think it is a pivotal factor
   for White functionality and livewire?

   _____

   _____

   _____

   _____

   _____

   _____

   _____

   _____

   _____

3. As an antiracist how can you ask racists to warm up to
   changing their minds on racism when they have a closed
   up mind and reluctance to change?

   _____

   _____

   _____

   _____

   _____

   _____

   _____

- **Action steps**
  1. Cleanse your mind of the wrong notions of antiracism. Pick
     up the right ideals and run with it.
- **Checklist**
  1. Racism is terminal but can be cured.

CHAPTER 18: SURVIVAL

Kendi watched as his wife Sadiqa struggled with breast cancer which was believed to be common amongst women within the age of 40 although she was thirty-four. Sadiqa's experience revealed the true source of racist ideas to her husband; Kendi. It showed that ignorance and hate have got nothing to do with racist ideas but self-interest. The history of racist ideas began from the making of strong racist policies by the policymaker out of selfish-interest and then creates racist ideas to support the display of inequality in their policies as the commoners consume those racist ideas and respond with hate and ignorance.

Likening the above scenario to a cancer patient with a growing tumor is the same as treating racism and suppose that hate and ignorance will magically shrink as if a cancer patient's tumor shrinks just because it is been treated. Taking out hate and ignorance and forget about the underlying cause will only return the aforementioned and inequalities in full force, it is only a matter of time; they will return in maximum momentum. Educational and moral suasions have not only failed woefully, but it is also suicidal.

We need to pay more attention to racist policy alteration over mental change. That is the starting of ending racism, and then the others will follow and fall into place. It is these racist policies that opened the door to racist ideas. In 2017, Kendi founded and directed the "Antiracist Research and Policy Center" at the American University. The result of the research from racism's history and antiracism revealed that policy experts, scholars, advocates, and journalists made positive headway in replacing the racist policy with antiracist policies. This led Kendi to gather a team to look into the following;

1. The most critical and ostensibly intractable racial inequities.
2. Investigate racist policies responsible for racial inequity.
3. Renew antiracist policy correctives.
4. Spread the word on the research and policy correctives.
5. Participate in revolutionary campaigns that work with antiracist power in areas to introduce and examine those policy correctives before sending them out nationally and internationally.
6. They are to exemplify the steps to help destroy racial inequality in our spaces.
7. Accept that racial inequality is the challenge of bad policy and has got nothing to do with the people.
8. Recognize racial inequality in its entire intersections and manifestations.
9. Investigate and reveal the racist policies causing racial inequalities.
10. Develop antiracist policies that can erase racial inequality.
11. Identify the groups and individuals responsible for instituting antiracist policies.
12. Spread and educate people on the revealed antiracist policy correctives and racist policy.
13. Use antiracist power to induce the cruel racist policymakers to constitute the antiracist policy.

- **Lessons**
    1. Race and racism are power constructs of the contemporary world.
    2. The history of racist ideas began from the making of strong racist policies by the policymaker out of selfish-interest.
- **Issues surrounding the subject matter**
    1. Is it of a surety that hate and ignorance are the only reactions to racist ideas? If not what other reactions do you think there are?

_____

_____

_____

_____

_____

_____

_____

_____

_____

_____

    2. Can our world be really purged of racism and if yes, how?

_____

_____

_____

_____

_____

_____

_____

_____

- **Goals**

1. What are you doing to change racist policies that leads t
racial ideas?

_____

_____

_____

_____

_____

_____

_____

_____

_____

- **Action steps**
  1. Begin to research and enlighten others to help chang
     racist policies.
- **Checklist**
  1. Work at new and more effective antiracist conducts unt
     they work.

CONCLUSION

Racist policies are not everlasting; neither are racist ideas natural to humans. It is high time to end the racial color-blindness, inequality, segregation, oppression, and unfair policies that only favor White supremacists.

Racism is fast spreading and is a very lethal cancer ever known. There isn't any factor that categorically states that; one day racism will be eradicated and inequality will be a thing of the past. But one sure thing is the hope and tenacity required to keep pushing for racial freedom even in the face of hopelessness and massive oppression from racist.

We can give humanity a fair chance to live in unity and freedom forever.

CPSIA information can be obtained
at www.ICGtesting.com
Printed in the USA
LVHW081350100221
678939LV00031B/547

9 781952 663321